THE SCHOOL OF JOSEPH

Bishop Dr. Emmanuel D. Apau Jr.

THE SCHOOL OF JOSEPH

ISBN: 978-9988-2-4506-1

Cover Design: Graceland Products & Services
Editors: Salamatu Gyamera, Alfreda S. Grace, Bishop Dr. Emmanuel D. Apau Jr.

For further inquiries, contact the author on:
P. O. Box 951
Akim Oda, E/R
Ghana
Email: worldlightbishop@gmail.com

DEDICATION

This book is dedicated to all my mentors.

To all followers of Jesus Christ.

ACKNOWLEDGMENT

This book has come this far due to the assistance of many people who have contributed their time, talents, ideas, etc. I am grateful to the Dean and Vice President of New Life Bible College and Seminary, Dr. Sandy Haga, who played a supportive role in my life when I was a student in the seminary. I also thank Dr. Emmanuel Osunkoya for his help and advice in my research at the seminary. I thank Bishop Dr. Goad, New Life Ministries, Virginia and Dr. Woodard, for their spiritual support.

I am thankful to my Professor, Rev. Dr. I. Ray Berrian, my academic advisor and project supervisor, at the Berrian Bible Institute, USA.

To Basilea Amoah Tetteh, Sarah Agbehia, my big sisters and Deaconess Theresa Eghan who helped me to type most of these manuscripts, I am very grateful for you all.

I thank my Music director, Mr. Martin for all his support and encouragement. To all my brothers and sisters (both those in the Lord and biologically) for their wonderful love and support in all my life endeavors. Brethren, I am very grateful for you all, you have helped me to realize my dreams in this life.

To my wife, Angela G. Akyea, thank you for being by my side at times when things were difficult and for your hard work in making these books come to reality. You are the best wife. Sweetheart, God richly bless you.

To my parents, Mr. Stephen Oyinka Apau and Mrs. Mercy Darkwa Apau, thanks for your great love for me.

To all who supported me and this project financially and spiritually, I am so grateful. Thanks for your time, prayers, love, hospitability, financial assistance, many other forms of support, etc. God richly bless you all.

SPECIAL THANKS

Special thanks to my heavenly Father, God Almighty for His help and wisdom to put this book together.

CONTENT

INTRODUCTION

It's been more than twenty (20) years now since I first decided to live by faith. Since then, my life has been more glorious than I could ever have imagined it to be. I have seen more victories than I could count. But you need to know that those victories didn't come my way easily. They did not happen overnight. I won those victories because I held on to the Word of God and refused to let it go. Even when the Word didn't appear to be working, I kept on reading it, studying it, meditating on it for revelation and speaking it out that I may see results. *Ephesians 6:16 BSB "In addition to all this, take up the shield of faith, with which you can extinguish all the flaming arrows of the evil one."* With faith, you too can move from victory to victory, from health to health, from breakthrough to breakthrough, and from abundance to abundance. I encourage you to walk by faith because it is written that the just shall live by faith. You must keep feeding on the Word of God and walking by faith. This book, The School of Joseph, is for both the young and old, the preachers, apostles, prophets, evangelists, pastors and teachers, church leaders, and anyone who desires to have an intimate walk with the Lord.

Remember that, as a child of God, trials and tribulations are inevitable. You will face ups and downs, slavery, imprisonment, and many more. Even if you have not yet gone through your school of Joseph, know that the time for you to face your tests and trials will surely come. Remember to allow God to take the glory in every difficult situation. It is my prayer that this book will help you to become so consistent in your study of the Word of God that its power will explode in you. May all who read this book be elevated from their lowly state of life into the positions they were destined to hold. May someone be moved from disgrace to grace! May God move you from your current position into the state of a prince or princess of the kingdom! May this book be a blessing to your life, and may God give you the faith not to abort the vision but to move from victory to victory for the rest of your life. Amen and amen.

CHAPTER ONE

YOUR FAITH MUST BE TESTED BEFORE YOU ARE ACCEPTED

Many times, circumstances befall the righteous that they cannot understand. In those situations, they may even be moved to question God and ask "Why me, Lord?" Many people who love God and care about the things of God and even sacrifice their lives for God go through hard times. Yet, in those situations, remind yourself that just because you haven't been healed does not change the fact that God is a Healer, even The Great Physician. The fact that you have not received the money that you requested from God or seen the baby you have been asking God for does not change the fact that God is The Provider. Know that you must hold on to your faith in Him and He will come through for you. *Hebrews 11:1-2 NKJV says "Now faith is the substance of things hoped for, the evidence of things not seen. For by it the elders obtained a good testimony."* It says that faith is a substance of things; in other words, the combination of the things you have heard from God, through His Word, and the evidence of those things. This means that it is the testimony-in-advance of what you have heard. Even though you have not seen them, you believe.

If you have asked the Lord the question, "Why me?", the answer to your question is simply that your faith must be tested. If your faith is not tested, God cannot testify about your faith. It is your response to God's tests in your life that causes Him to add you to the fathers or people of faith in your generation.

Are You Prepared for The Test?

Unfortunately, the children of God are often not prepared for the tests and trials of life. But understand that even in the secular world those who don't prepare well for their exams at school must expect failure. While it is true that we are walking with the Lord, we must remain aware that God can and does allow certain tests to come our way and, for that reason, we must not allow them to take us by surprise. Who would have imaged that Joseph's own brothers could even think of killing him? Although God did prevent that from coming to pass, they developed another plan to sell him and succeeded with that plan. God allowed it to succeed to test his faith and to teach us a lesson today. Can you imagine having to endure a severe challenge in your life that comes your way because of the doing of your family members or your best friends? That is also the reason why the Bible warns us not to put our trust in man. The Lord says in *Jeremiah 17:5 NKJV "Cursed is the man who trusts in man And makes flesh his strength, Whose heart departs from the LORD."* And again in *Matthew 10:36 BSB "A man's enemies will be the members of his own household."* As a child of God, remain prepared for your test because one thing that is certain is that you will be tested. And the purpose of the test is to prove that your faith is alive and working.

James 2:14-17 NKJV, "What does it profit, my brethren, if someone says he has faith but does not have works? Can faith save him? If a brother or sister is naked and destitute of daily food, and one of you says to them, "Depart in peace, be warmed and filled," but you do not give them the things which are needed for the body, what does it profit? Thus also faith by itself, if it does not have works, is dead."

The Word Will Prove or Test You

Psalm 105:16-19 NKJV
"Moreover He called for a famine in the land; He destroyed all the provision of bread. He sent a man before them—Joseph—who was sold as a slave. They hurt his feet with fetters, He was laid in irons. Until the time that his word came to pass, The word of the Lord tested him.

The question is, why must someone who has received such a prophetic word from the Lord go through all these trials, such as shame, disgrace, and tests? One would think that, if God has made him a promise, things should have been easy for him. Yet, they weren't. This is simply to show us that our ways are not the ways of God and our thoughts are not His thoughts. His ways and thoughts are superior in comparison with ours.

The Will of God

Although the things Joseph went through were not pleasant, it was the will of God concerning his life. It was part of the package of his greatness. The scriptures say that He (God) sent a man ahead of them, Joseph, who was sold as a slave. How could the carrier of the promise become a slave? Where was God at such a time? Could He not deliver Joseph and spare him from all that disgrace? They bruised his feet with shackles. In other words, his feet were chained like a criminal and his neck was in an iron collar. Yet, he was the promised candidate. How could the person, who God Himself has promised, go through all those calamities? Understand that the prophetic word of God upon your life will expose you to tests yet God knows that you will be able to pass those tests. The tests may be rough, tough, and twisted, yet, they will work for your good. *Romans 8:28 NLT "And we know that God causes everything to work together for the good of those who love God and are called according to his purpose for them."*

Jesus Was Tested

The truth is that no child of God is above being tested. As long as you call yourself a son or a daughter of God, you will face some tests. Even Jesus Christ, who was born by the Holy Spirit and through the virgin Mary, had to go through tests. The tests came because the anointing (or the prophetic word) upon His life exposed Him to be tested. The purpose of the anointing (or prophetic word) upon your life is for you to accomplish a specific task. Every kingdom-anointing has been issued to complete a specific task and that anointing will be challenged by the devil in accordance with the permissive will of God. So, you must understand that every prophetic word upon your life is already under attack by the enemy.

Three (3) Areas of Testing
Every test falls within the following three categories. No one will endure a test apart from these three areas.
1. The lust of the flesh

2. The lust of the eyes
3. The pride of life

1 John 2:15-17 NLT

"Do not love this world nor the things it offers you, for when you love the world, you do not have the love of the Father in you. For the world offers only a craving for physical pleasure, a craving for everything we see, and pride in our achievements and possessions. These are not from the Father, but are from this world. And this world is fading away, along with everything that people crave. But anyone who does what pleases God will live forever."

Luke 4:1-13 NKJV

Then Jesus, being filled with the Holy Spirit, returned from the Jordan and was led by the Spirit into the wilderness, being tempted for forty days by the devil. And in those days He ate nothing, and afterward, when they had ended, He was hungry. And the devil said to Him, "If You are the Son of God, command this stone to become bread." But Jesus answered him, saying, "It is written, 'Man shall not live by bread alone, but by every word of God.' " Then the devil, taking Him up on a high mountain, showed Him all the kingdoms of the world in a moment of time. And the devil said to Him, "All this authority I will give You, and their glory; for this has been delivered to me, and I give it to whomever I wish. Therefore, if You will worship before me, all will be Yours."

And Jesus answered and said to him, "Get behind Me, Satan! For it is written, 'You shall worship the Lord your God, and Him only you shall serve.' " Then he brought Him to Jerusalem, set Him on the pinnacle of the temple, and said to Him, "If You are the Son of God, throw Yourself down from here. For it is written: 'He shall give His angels charge over you,
To keep you,'and, 'In their hands they shall bear you up, Lest you dash your foot against a stone.' " And Jesus answered and said to him, "It has been said, 'You shall not tempt the Lord your God.' " Now when the devil

had ended every temptation, he departed from Him until an opportune time."

Notice, in this scripture, that the Devil quoted from *Psalm 91*. He, being fully aware of the lust of the flesh, had hoped that the Lord Jesus Christ would fall into his trap just as he entrapped the first Adam to do. Secondly, we see the test in the area of the lust of the eye because the devil showed him the kingdom and said, "if you will worship me, it will all be yours". This is the way that the devil often enslaves the children of man, by offering us what looks pleasant to the eye to rob us of our true worship to the Lord.

Lastly, we see the test in the area of the pride of life when the devil asked Jesus to throw himself that he may be carried by the angels. He thought he could entrap the King of Kings with the appearance of high regard and esteem, which the people of this world seek after and cherish greatly. Yet, the scripture says concerning Him, that he had already *"…emptied himself, by taking the form of a servant, being born in the likeness of men." Philippians 2:7 ESV.*

Matthew 6:31-33 "Therefore do not worry, saying, 'What shall we eat?' or 'What shall we drink?' or 'What shall we wear?' 32For after all these things the Gentiles seek. For your heavenly Father knows that you need all these things. 33But seek first the kingdom of God and His righteousness, and all these things shall be added to you."

Remember that any test you face will fall within one of these three areas.
Lust of the Flesh: What the body craves
Lust of the Eyes: What the eyes crave
Pride of Life: What you possess

The devil can only be stopped by your obedience to God as you feed yourself with His Word. Every word of God that you use against Satan bruises him since the Word of God is the Sword of the Spirit (Heb 4:12, Eph 6:12).

Note that Joseph was one of the representations for Jesus in the Old

Testament. There were several similarities between them. They both were hated because of the grace of God (the anointing) upon their lives. They were both wrongly accused. They both received a punishment that they did not deserve. They were betrayed by their own brothers or close friends, and endured shame and disgrace, etc.. Despite these setbacks and trials, they passed their tests.

Everyone Will Be Tested

Job 14:1 KJV "Man that is born of a woman is of few days, and full of trouble."
Psalm 34:19 KJV "Many are the afflictions of the righteous: but the LORD delivereth him out of them all."

Do not be deceived, whatever your case may be, you will be tested; but, remember that you must pass the test. Even if you are already grown or have become an old minister without having gone through any major tests or what I call "the school of Joseph" in your life, remember that you will face that test at some point in your lifetime. The "School of Joseph" is one or several major trials, tests, tribulations, or afflictions that the Lord permits us to endure.

Some people have their test at an early stage of their ministry or life, others in the middle stages of their ministry or life, while others experience theirs at the later part of their ministry or life. Some people go through their tests from time to time. Yet, in every case, they serve the purpose of strengthening us and our faith and make us stronger in our walk with the Lord.

James 1:2-40 NKJV "My brethren, count it all joy when you fall into various trials, knowing that the testing of your faith produces patience. But let patience have its perfect work, that you may be perfect and complete, lacking nothing."

These trials of many kinds that we face in the ministry exist to test our faith. They are simply situations and circumstances that need to occur for you to prove your faith and to test whether you truly believe the word that God has spoken to you.

Some people only praise God and are joyful when things go well; but, in all your trials and temptations, remember to count it all joy. Again, remember to count it pure joy. Consider each situation that you go through. Each should reveal to you that the Lord is with you and that the anointing of God rests upon you.

CHAPTER TWO

THE ANOINTING EXPOSES YOU

The anointing of God will expose you to the world; both, the physical and the spiritual world. You immediately become a threat to satanic powers, evil spirits, and to the devil himself from the day God anoints you.

One of the things the devil is afraid of is the anointing. So, if you are anointed by the Lord, he will bring anything he can into your life to rob you or kill that anointing. Potiphar's wife tempted Joseph to sleep with her so that his anointing will be taken from him. Likewise, the devil will try to strip you of your anointing. Jesus was tempted so that he may be emptied of his anointing, but we thank God that the devil could not stand him.

The devil cannot touch the anointing, or the unction, because it is the power of God. Therefore, he cannot touch His anointed. For this reason, he will rather try to bring things your way in hopes of emptying you of your anointing. Remember that it is written, God said, *"Do not touch My anointed ones, And do My prophets no harm." (1 Chronicles 16:22 NKJV; Psalm 105:15 NKJV).*

Respect the Anointing

Respect the anointing of God because God has commanded, "do not touch my anointed". If you are the anointed of the Lord, you are surely blessed because no one can touch you nor your house or your children or even your properties, except by the permission of God or when the Lord Himself removes the hedges from your life. That is why you must remember to ask for His anointing; because, with the presence and anointing, you can reach where the Lord has purposed to take you.

The scripture says, *"When they went from one nation to another, And from one kingdom to another people, He permitted no man to do them wrong; Yes, He rebuked kings for their sakes, Saying, "Do not touch My anointed ones, And do My prophets no harm." 1 Chronicles 16:20-22*

NKJV. The anointing can break any undue protocol and lift you up despite many hindrances and setbacks. Remember how God's anointing broke the protocol of Egypt and qualified Joseph to become prime minister although he had been a slave and even a prisoner. Recall how this same anointing of God broke the laws of nature so that Shadrach, Meshach, and Abednego were not burned in the furnace, although the temperature had been raised to its hottest? Praise God! That is why the devil is envious of your anointing and wants to strip you of it. He cannot touch it himself so he will bring things into your life that, if you are not vigilant, will strip you of it.

Do Not Touch My Anointed and Do My Prophets No Harm

Beloved, you cannot be touched and you cannot be harmed. When the anointed lift up their voices, the devil takes to flight because the anointing breaks or destroys yokes.

Isaiah 10:27 NKJV
"It shall come to pass in that day
That his burden will be taken away from your shoulder,
And his yoke from your neck,
And the yoke will be destroyed because of the anointing oil.

Anointing

It is the anointing that lifts burdens, breaks yokes, protocols, and shackles of iron and bronze in the realm of the Spirit. It is the anointing that destroys the works of the devil. It is the anointing that heals the sick, raises the dead and casts out devils. The anointing brings good things. That is why the devil hates the anointed. He saw the anointing upon Jesus' life and wanted to destroy it; but, thanks be to God, he could not touch the anointed one (the Lord).

Acts 10:38 KJV "How God anointed Jesus of Nazareth with the Holy Ghost and with power: who went about doing good, and healing all that were oppressed of the devil; for God was with him."

Luke 4:14-15 NKJV "Then Jesus returned in the power of the Spirit to Galilee, and news of Him went out through all the surrounding region. And He taught in their synagogues, being glorified by all."

Luke 4:18-19 NKJV "The Spirit of the Lord is upon Me, Because He has anointed Me To preach the gospel to the poor; He has sent Me to heal the brokenhearted, To proclaim liberty to the captives And recovery of sight to the blind, To set at liberty those who are oppressed; To proclaim the acceptable year of the Lord."

The anointing prospers and the devil hates the anointed. So, for the rest of your life, as long as you are the anointed of the Lord, you will constantly engage in a battle with the enemy; but thank God that you are untouchable and cannot be harmed by him as long as you keep yourself from being stripped of the anointing.

You are the Joseph of your days! Do not allow the devil to empty your anointing tank. Do not allow him because the anointing is precious. Yet, know that the mere fact that you will not allow him to strip you of your anointing doesn't mean that you are free from facing challenges. Joseph did not allow the woman to sleep with him. Yet, for that very reason, he was accused of rape and it caused him to be sent to prison. The same can happen to you. Know that there are many people who have paid for the wrong they have not committed; but thank God that, even while Joseph was in prison, the anointing remained upon him. The presence and anointing of the Lord were not imprisoned but were there with him to deliver him from the prison. Praise God!

1 Peter 3:13-14 NKJV "And who is he who will harm you if you become followers of what is good? But even if you should suffer for righteousness' sake, you are blessed. "And do not be afraid of their threats, nor be troubled."

Acts 7:9-10 NKJV "And the patriarchs, becoming envious, sold Joseph into Egypt. But God was with him and delivered him out of all his troubles, and gave him favor and wisdom in the presence of Pharaoh, king of Egypt; and he made him governor over Egypt and all his house."

Do Not Trade In Your Anointing

As a Christian, you will come to a point where you will face the choice of exchanging or substituting your anointing. Trading in your anointing is when you substitute your God-given destiny with what Satan or the world presents to you. It happened to Abraham. Had God not been a God of covenant, Abraham could have exchanged Isaac for Ishmael. The same thing happened to Lot and his family; Lot's wife exchanged her salvation for her vain possession. Likewise, Esau traded his birthright for food. Likewise, even the first Adam exchanged his destiny for death. But Christ Jesus is our perfect example. Although the devil challenged him to trade his anointing, our Lord Jesus Christ held on to the Word and defeated the devil (Matthew 4:1-11, 2 Timothy 2:13) because He was the Word Himself. Remember that you are the Joseph of this generation; do not allow your gift to be exchanged for the futile riches of the enemy or the devilish things of this world. Keep in mind that all of you, God's people, will be challenged by the enemy because he is looking for someone who will be enticed to exchange their anointing for the things of the world. However, with the Word of God, you can resist him. Beloved, tell the devil now that enough is enough and take a stand for the sake of your destiny. That counterfeit lion is looking for you but you can, yes you can, stop him by the Word of God.

1 Peter 5:8-9 NKJV "Be sober, be vigilant; because your adversary the devil walks about like a roaring lion, seeking whom he may devour. Resist him, steadfast in the faith, knowing that the same sufferings are experienced by your brotherhood in the world."

CHAPTER THREE

ALL GOD'S PEOPLE WILL BE TESTED
(School of Joseph)

From Genesis to Revelation, you can see that every man and woman of God has gone through trials, tests, temptations, etc. and they received their testimonies according to their personal experiences with God. Yet, all who depended on the strength of God survived by the name of the Lord. It began from the time of the first Adam. He faced his test but failed because he made a choice which resulted in his death, both physical and spiritual. Do your best to pass your test because, whenever you fail, you must start again and again; and sometimes, it becomes harder each time. The first Adam failed his test, but the Second Adam, who is Christ Jesus, has given us the power and ability to stand in any test we face. Hallelujah! The tests come in various ways to different individuals. Cain and Abel were tested. In Noah's time, they received their test. Abraham had his own and passed the test of faith. But, the test involving Ishmael became a problem for him. Isaac had his own test and he was further challenged when the Philistines fought him about the well that his own father had dug. Jacob and Esau had their own tests. You need to remember that every trial that comes your way has a purpose.

Joseph's test was tough and, yet, he passed. Moses also had his test as a young man when he met the Lord. He went through tough times with the Israelites, but he was able to stand. Joshua also experienced his tests. He made a covenant with the Gibeonites without first consulting God. All the Judges each had their own tests. All the prophets had theirs. The early church also faced their tests. No one in the Bible, nor even in this present world, whom the Lord has lifted up has gone without tests because the testing of your faith produces perseverance. You must allow your faith to carry you to the point where God can raise you up. It is through your test that you will get your testimony.

Hebrew 11:32-40 (KJV),

32 "And what shall I more say? for the time would fail me to tell of Gedeon, and of Barak, and of Samson, and of Jephthae; of David also, and Samuel, and of the prophets:

33 Who through faith subdued kingdoms, wrought righteousness, obtained promises, stopped the mouths of lions.

34 Quenched the violence of fire, escaped the edge of the sword, out of weakness were made strong, waxed valiant in fight, turned to flight the armies of the aliens.

35 Women received their dead raised to life again: and others were tortured, not accepting deliverance; that they might obtain a better resurrection:

36 And others had trial of cruel mockings and scourgings, yea, moreover of bonds and imprisonment:

37 They were stoned, they were sawn asunder, were tempted, were slain with the sword: they wandered about in sheepskins and goatskins; being destitute, afflicted, tormented;

38 (Of whom the world was not worthy:) they wandered in deserts, and in mountains, and in dens and caves of the earth.

39 And these all, having obtained a good report through faith, received not the promise:

40 God having provided some better thing for us, that they without us should not be made perfect.

All these men endured hardship as a form of discipline. When you are disciplined by God, remember that God is treating you as His child. It is written in *Hebrews 12:7 BSB, "If you endure discipline, God is treating you as sons; for what son is there whom his father does not discipline?"* If you are not disciplined and, yet, everyone else undergoes discipline, then you are illegitimate children and not true sons. God disciplines us for our good so that we may share in His holiness.

Also, remember that *Hebrews 12:11-13 BSB* says *"No discipline seems enjoyable at the time, but painful. Later on, however, it yields a peaceful harvest of righteousness to those who have been trained by it. Therefore strengthen your limp hands and weak knees. Make straight paths for your feet, so that the lame may not be debilitated, but rather healed."* All these men and women of God endured several trials which were very tough. It shaped them, trained them, and caused them to become productive in the areas that God wanted to use their lives.

Don't Be Discourage When Trials Come Your Way

Even in your attacks, remember that God is still with you. God encourages us to "fear not" many times in the Bible. Each day when you wake up, read one "fear not" just like the people who take daily prescription pills do and remember that, even in your deepest darkest hour, the Lord is still your light. Don't think too much about or dwell on things that will not benefit you; but, in your attacks, fix your eyes on Jesus, the author and finisher of your faith. In Joseph's test, he did not become discouraged because he knew within his heart that he had not sinned against God and that was enough for him.

Many people likely said many evil things to him. It is possible that people said or wrote terrible things concerning him or even taunted him, calling him the "Hebrew slave boy" or young man who wanted to sleep with his master's wife. Imagine how you would have felt if it were you. Would you have questioned God, asking, "Why me, God?"

If it was truly the Lord who gave Joseph those promises, why then was he facing those terrible challenges? Was the Lord asleep while he suffered these things? Yet, we know that our God does not sleep nor slumber. One thing I want you to know is that the Lord was with Joseph, even while he was in prison. It doesn't matter if all you were doing was standing for the truth and yet you were still accused of wrongdoing, you must know that God is still with you regardless of where you are and where you have been placed. They put Joseph in prison, yet, the Lord was with him. So, you must remember that God will never leave you nor forsake you.

Joseph encouraged himself in the Lord and found his strength in the Lord because he knew that the Lord was his strength and his song, even while he was in chains and in prison. Have you been wrongly accused for standing for the truth? Remember that the truth cannot be buried. The truth will speak in the end. Do not give up on your Lord simply because men have risen against you. Continue to remember your first love for the Lord.

Hebrew 10:32-39 KJV, "32 But call to remembrance the former days, in which, after ye were illuminated, ye endured a great fight of afflictions;

33 Partly, whilst ye were made a gazingstock both by reproaches and afflictions; and partly, whilst ye became companions of them that were so used.

34 For ye had compassion of me in my bonds, and took joyfully the spoiling of your goods, knowing in yourselves that ye have in heaven a better and an enduring substance.

35 Cast not away therefore your confidence, which hath great recompence of reward.

36 For ye have need of patience, that, after ye have done the will of God, ye might receive the promise.

37 For yet a little while, and he that shall come will come, and will not tarry.

38 Now the just shall live by faith: but if any man draw back, my soul shall have no pleasure in him.

39 But we are not of them who draw back unto perdition; but of them that believe to the saving of the soul."

Do not become discouraged nor stop along the way. Encourage yourself in the Lord. Don't throw or cast away your confidence for it has a great reward. God will reward you for not shrinking back. If you allow discouragement to set in and stop you, you will continue to die gradually in the things you do in the name of God and you will not receive your reward. Although you may have been exposed to public insults, or persecution, etc., remember that the joy of the Lord is your strength.

CHAPTER FOUR

THREE THINGS MINISTERS SHOULD BE CAREFUL OF

Below are three things that every child of God must be very careful about:
1. Women/Men
2. Money
3. Pride

Women/Men:

Every minister, especially the young ministers must be careful of women. This is especially important if you're a man because the devil has used women to bring down many men of God. Remember that even a mighty man like King David was brought down by a woman and even a wise man like King Solomon, turned his heart against God and served other gods because of his lust after women.

In the book of Numbers 25, the Moabite women seduced Israel and 24,000 soldiers of Israel were killed by the Lord as a result. So you must remember that the relationship between men and women is a very powerful one. If you are a young minister, be careful about your relationship with women or men. I urge the male ministers to be especially alert.

Women of God must also be careful about their relationship with men and remember that if you are not careful in this area it can completely hinder your ministry or destiny. The devil knows this very well and has been using it as a tool especially against the men of God. Remember how the devil used Potiphar's wife against Joseph. Likewise, the devil can use women against you and your ministry. Keep in mind that he can use any woman or man, regardless of where you encounter them. He can even use the women in the church to bring you down. I have seen the devil rise against many young ministers of God to a point that they could no longer continue their journey. In many of those cases, the very weapon that the devil used was the lust after women or men.

Are there women disturbing you in your church, in your prayer group, or even in your youth ministry, intending to sleep with you? Recognize that it is the spirit of lust at work. Lust works in many people in the church today. Do not give them the chance because sexual sin will usher you into a covenant that is not easily broken. Because of such covenants, it is advisable for young ministers to marry a virgin prepared by the Lord.

Potiphar's wife attacked Joseph's life and was a threat against his ministry, but the power of the Lord was strong upon him to deliver him. Don't deceive yourself and mistake a sinful temptation for a blessing or an opportunity in disguise. It will deplete you of your anointing and hinder your ministry. Unless the strong hand of God delivers you, you may even lose your ministry. Joseph was able to flee, praise God.

Flee From Sexual Sin

1 Corinthians 6:15-20 KJV
15 Know ye not that your bodies are the members of Christ? shall I then take the members of Christ, and make them the members of an harlot? God forbid.
16 What? know ye not that he which is joined to an harlot is one body? for two, saith he, shall be one flesh.
17 But he that is joined unto the Lord is one spirit.
18 Flee fornication. Every sin that a man doeth is without the body; but he that committeth fornication sinneth against his own body.
19 What? know ye not that your body is the temple of the Holy Ghost which is in you, which ye have of God, and ye are not your own?
20 For ye are bought with a price: therefore glorify God in your body, and in your spirit, which are God's.

Your body is very important to God so you must not treat it anyhow nor misuse it. Today, many regard sex as if it is a game that must be played. People do all manner of things with their bodies and then appear before the Lord with the same body they have defiled. People go to church but have boyfriends and girlfriends (or boy-lovers and girl-lovers, as I call it), but not according to the will of the Lord. They don't desire to marry according to the will of God, yet they fornicate. They defile their bodies and forfeit their spiritual covering. I urge you not to engage in sexual sin. Even marriage is not about sex, but about oneness. People desire sex, but they don't desire to share their lives in marriage. They fail to realize that, according to the scriptures, anytime two people sleep together, they already share their lives, whether they like it or not, because blood is life (Leviticus 17). So, I urge you to not entertain them; they will only cause your downfall.

Young men and women, God commands you to flee from sexual sin. Joseph fled and you also need to flee. It doesn't matter how strong or high you feel the level of anointing upon your life is. I urge you not to play with sexual sin. Flee from it, because it has great consequences. Joseph fled so that he could maintain his peace with God. The Lord has said that you become one with whomever you sleep with. This means that if the person is possessed, you automatically become possessed too because you become one flesh with them. Anyone that commits sexual sin sins against their own body. Your body is the temple of the Holy Ghost and, moreover, you have been bought with a high price. So you must value the price that was paid for you (the blood of Jesus Christ) and separate yourself from all sexual sin.

Hebrew 10:26-31 NKJV
"26 For if we sin willfully after we have received the knowledge of the truth, there no longer remains a sacrifice for sins,
27 but a certain fearful expectation of judgment, and fiery indignation which will devour the adversaries.
28 Anyone who has rejected Moses' law dies without mercy on the testimony of *two or three witnesses.*
29 Of how much worse punishment, do you suppose, will he be thought worthy who has trampled the Son of God underfoot, counted the blood of the covenant by which he was sanctified a common thing, and insulted the Spirit of grace?
30 For we know Him who said, "Vengeance is Mine, I will repay," says the Lord. And again, "The Lord will judge His people."
31 It is a fearful thing to fall into the hands of the living God."

You must value the blood that purchased you. If you play with it, it will be required of you. Realize that you were precious enough to the Lord that He gave His own son for your body, soul, and your spirit. It is the body that carries the spirit and the soul so you must show respect to God by honoring your body and staying away from sexual sin.

Money:

1Timothy 6:10-12 KJV
"10 For the love of money is the root of all evil: which while some coveted after, they have erred from the faith, and pierced themselves through with many sorrows.
11 But thou, O man of God, flee these things; and follow after righteousness, godliness, faith, love, patience, meekness.
12 Fight the good fight of faith, lay hold on eternal life, whereunto thou art also called, and hast professed a good profession before many witnesses."

I believe that Joseph could have had everything, as far as money was concerned. Yet, he chose prison instead of the money. Potiphar's wife failed to entice him and may have even given up on him because his eyes were fixed on the Lord. Has someone offered you money? Check the motives behind it before accepting it or else, at the end, it may only bring you trouble. Joseph could have had everything, materially speaking, in Potiphar's house; but accepting the riches of the devil could have caused him to lose what God desired for him. He may have never become the prime minister and his family could have died during the time of the famine; but, because of his love for the Lord, he was able to stand firm to reject the illegitimate promotions that Potiphar's wife offered him.

While I am not suggesting that you reject every gift when God prompts the hearts of certain individuals to give to you, I am telling you to be careful because not everyone has good intentions, although they may pretend as if they are giving you gifts from a pure heart.

These are lessons that I was able to learn from, by the grace of God. So, I am giving you the wisdom I have gained that you may be able to avoid trouble before it comes near. Often, many gifts are not gifts from God but are rather traps for unsuspecting individuals. Know that whatever Potiphar's wife offered to Joseph was not truly a gift at all. No good gift from God will cause you to fall into sin. Every good and perfect gift comes from heaven from God, in whom there is no shadow of turning.

I remember a lady who came to a church pretending to have a desire to devote herself to the things of God. She eventually confessed that she was only working hard because she was looking for a husband. This happens often, to both men and women. Some people do things for the glory of God while others do it for personal reasons. Therefore, pray for God to help you to discern the motives behind whatever people offer to you. Everything that Potiphar's wife offered Joseph was offered with evil motives behind it. This woman gave Joseph her own body to fulfill her desires. If you were in Joseph's position, would you have considered yourself lucky, or blessed with a "scholarship" as I like to call it? Joseph was able to resist her because he loved God. Your love for God will deliver you from many sins that lead to destruction. Never substitute your grace and ministry for money, or women and men. Praise God.

Pride:

Pride is the act of exalting oneself. One thing that God hates is pride because it reminds Him of the devil who is the father of pride. The devil, full of pride, once even said that he will exalt his throne above the Most High.

Isaiah 14:13-14 NLT
"For you said to yourself,
'I will ascend to heaven and set my throne above God's stars.
I will preside on the mountain of the gods
far away in the north.
I will climb to the highest heavens
and be like the Most High.'

Do not allow your heart to be overtaken by pride. Again, beware of pride. In the kingdom of God, if you desire to be elevated, you must first come down (or humble yourself) and God will lift you up. In the world, it is the lowly that serve the great, but in God, it is the great that serve the lowly. That is why Jesus told His disciples to humble themselves and become like little children if they desire to become great in the kingdom of God.

Evil Competition is Vain

There is no need to compete with anyone in God's kingdom. Refrain from competing with your leader, your pastors, or anyone at all because their grace is different from yours. You only need to do what God has asked you to do and to do it faithfully according to the gifts He has given to you. While you can learn from others, praise God for their lives, and add what you learn from them to improve yours, you must refrain from competing with them because, as long as you don't possess their gifts, you cannot operate like them. There must rather be a division of labor and specialization. That way, God alone will be glorified. Do all that you can and do it wholeheartedly. Do not allow pride to set in. In your service for God, you must hate pride.

James 4:6-10 KJV
"6 But he giveth more grace. Wherefore he saith, God resisteth the proud, but giveth grace unto the humble.
7 Submit yourselves therefore to God. Resist the devil, and he will flee from you.
8 Draw nigh to God, and he will draw nigh to you. Cleanse your hands, ye sinners; and purify your hearts, ye double minded.
9 Be afflicted, and mourn, and weep: let your laughter be turned to mourning, and your joy to heaviness.
10 Humble yourselves in the sight of the Lord, and he shall lift you up."

Humility is the key to enter into the presence of God. Verse 7 of this scripture says, *"So humble yourself before God, Resist the devil, and he will flee from you" (James 4:7, NLT)*. Humility is also your power to resist Satan.

So, these are the three things (men or women, money, and pride) that the men and women of God (especially the younger ministers) must remain careful about. If any young minister falls from grace, it is usually because they have fallen in one of these areas.

Prayer

I pray that God will deliver you from every trap that can cause you pain in your ministry or hinder the growth of your ministry, in Jesus' name. Amen and amen. May His hand deliver you from every kind of carnality. May His hand protect you from adulterous men and women. May every agent of the devil, sent into your life to attack your ministry or bring shame to God, catch fire and may they be forced to return in shame to wherever they came from, in Jesus' mighty name.

CHAPTER FIVE

ALL ATTACKS COME BECAUSE OF YOUR DREAM

Genesis 37.1 NKJV
1 Now Jacob dwelt in the land where his father was a stranger, in the land of Canaan. 2 This is the history of Jacob.

Joseph, being seventeen years old, was feeding the flock with his brothers. And the lad was with the sons of Bilhah and the sons of Zilpah, his father's wives; and Joseph brought a bad report of them to his father.

3 Now Israel loved Joseph more than all his children, because he was the son of his old age. Also he made him a tunic of many colors. 4 But when his brothers saw that their father loved him more than all his brothers, they hated him and could not speak peaceably to him.

5 Now Joseph had a dream, and he told it to his brothers; and they hated him even more. 6 So he said to them, "Please hear this dream which I have dreamed: 7 There we were, binding sheaves in the field. Then behold, my sheaf arose and also stood upright; and indeed your sheaves stood all around and bowed down to my sheaf."

8 And his brothers said to him, "Shall you indeed reign over us? Or shall you indeed have dominion over us?" So they hated him even more for his dreams and for his words.

9 Then he dreamed still another dream and told it to his brothers, and said, "Look, I have dreamed another dream. And this time, the sun, the moon, and the eleven stars bowed down to me."

10 So he told it to his father and his brothers; and his father rebuked him and said to him, "What is this dream that you have dreamed? Shall your mother and I and your brothers indeed come to bow down to the earth before you?" 11 And his brothers envied him, but his father kept the matter in mind.

12 Then his brothers went to feed their father's flock in Shechem. 13 And Israel said to Joseph, "Are not your brothers feeding the flock in Shechem? Come, I will send you to them."

So he said to him, "Here I am."

14 Then he said to him, "Please go and see if it is well with your brothers and well with the flocks, and bring back word to me." So he sent him out of the Valley of Hebron, and he went to Shechem.

15 Now a certain man found him, and there he was, wandering in the field. And the man asked him, saying, "What are you seeking?"

16 So he said, "I am seeking my brothers. Please tell me where they are feeding their flocks."

17 And the man said, "They have departed from here, for I heard them say, 'Let us go to Dothan.' " So Joseph went after his brothers and found them in Dothan.

18 Now when they saw him afar off, even before he came near them, they conspired against him to kill him. 19 Then they said to one another, "Look, this dreamer is coming! 20 Come therefore, let us now kill him and cast him into some pit; and we shall say, 'Some wild beast has devoured him.' We shall see what will become of his dreams!"

21 But Reuben heard it, and he delivered him out of their hands, and said, "Let us not kill him." 22 And Reuben said to them, "Shed no blood, but cast him into this pit which is in the wilderness, and do not lay a hand on him"—that he might deliver him out of their hands, and bring him back to his father."

Why Did Joseph Go Through Attacks

There is always a reason behind the attacks you face. According to the scriptures, Joseph was a dreamer and he faced many attacks because of his dreams. The question is, do you have a dream? If so, then be prepared to be attacked. Your dream will cause you to have many enemies. Anyone who lacks the spirit of God will not be happy to see your progress. Even those with the spirit of God can become envious of you when they don't see the same things happening in their own lives. Do you remember how Joseph's brothers began attacking him because of his dreams? They didn't want him to rule over them, but the truth is that whatever God has purposed will come to pass and no one will be able to change it.

Joseph's dream indicated that he would rise above his brothers and peers and they didn't like that. Be aware that the enemy doesn't want you to rise above him and that is why he has made it his mission to work against your life. Your enemies always want you to be inferior to them or in a position of dependence upon them. So when your eyes are opened and you can see what the Lord sees, or, in other words, when you confirm what God has said concerning your life, they begin to fight against you. Everything that comes to pass or is accomplished starts with a vision. Sometimes, our visions are not in alignment with God's purpose and plan for us. At times, what you envision may be contrary to what God has for you. The question is, do you see what the Lord sees? We must make it our prayer to the Lord that His will for our lives may be done on earth as it is in heaven. *Matthew 6:9-10 NKJV, "In this manner, therefore, pray: Our Father in heaven, Hallowed be Your name. Your kingdom come. Your will be done On earth as* it is *in heaven"*.

How do you view yourself? Do you view yourself as a failure or as a successful person in the Lord? Do you see yourself as a lender or a borrower? Do you see blessings or curses? Do you see or envision your children being blessed or cursed? What you see is very important. You must see through the eyes of God and see what God sees. Joseph saw God's plan for his life. He saw himself being raised up. The fact that God had a plan for him, the fact that he could see that plan clearly, and his act of sharing it all called for an attack. So, you must also be very careful of whom you share your dreams with as well as the time and place you share it. You must always seek the face of the Lord before sharing your dreams and visions with others. Attacks will always come; yes, even after seeking the face of the Lord before sharing your dreams and visions with others. However, seeking the face of the Lord will help you to be prepared to face the attacks victoriously when they come. Joseph saw greatness; the moon and the stars were all bowing to him. Today, I pray that you will open your eyes and begin to see through the eyes of the Holy Ghost.

Genesis 37:5-11 NKJV

5 Now Joseph had a dream, and he told it to his brothers; and they hated him even more. 6 So he said to them, "Please hear this dream which I have dreamed: 7 There we were, binding sheaves in the field. Then behold, my sheaf arose and also stood upright; and indeed your sheaves stood all around and bowed down to my sheaf."

8 And his brothers said to him, "Shall you indeed reign over us? Or shall you indeed have dominion over us?" So they hated him even more for his dreams and for his words.

9 Then he dreamed still another dream and told it to his brothers, and said, "Look, I have dreamed another dream. And this time, the sun, the moon, and the eleven stars bowed down to me."

10 So he told it to his father and his brothers; and his father rebuked him and said to him, "What is this dream that you have dreamed? Shall your mother and I and your brothers indeed come to bow down to the earth before you?" 11 And his brothers envied him, but his father kept the matter in mind.

Joseph Confirms His Dream

Another thing that brought attacks upon Joseph's life was the fact that he confessed his dream. Whenever you confirm what you see, it exposes you to the enemy. You confirm the vision when you agree with it wholeheartedly with your spirit, soul, and body, and subsequently, take a stand for it and begin to take steps towards it. The enemy does not want you to confirm your dream. The devil becomes envious of you because he knows that you're about to give birth to new things that will bring glory to God. The devil wants you to be an aimless person walking about without knowing where you are going. He wants you to be a man without a purpose. As soon as Joseph shared his dreams with his father and brothers, they hated him the more. Know that if they will not rejoice with you, then automatically, they will hate you.

Anyone that cannot rejoice with you about the good things the Lord is doing in your life is not your supporter. The brothers knew the power of confession, so as they heard and saw Joseph confirm his dreams, they planned to kill the dream with their hatred, anger, rage, lack of concern for his life, etc.

The Vision-Killers

Some people are vision-killers. Most of the time, the vision-killers are members of your own household or even your closest friends. It is often the ones who are the closest to you that will betray you. Joseph's own brothers were his vision-killers. Anyone who rises against your God-given dream is your vision-killer. Potiphar's wife was another one of his vision-killers.

Remember that only you can fulfill the assignment that the Lord has for you so you must not allow anyone to kill it. It is written in *Jeremiah 1:11-12 NKJV*, *"Moreover the word of the Lord came to me, saying, "Jeremiah, what do you see?" And I said, "I see a branch of an almond tree." Then the Lord said to me, "You have seen well, for I am ready to perform My word."*

Anything that wants to kill your vision, can kill you as well. For example, Joseph's own brothers suddenly considered killing him in order to kill his vision. They said to themselves, "here is the dreamer, let us kill him and see if his dream will come to pass". Because of your dreams, they would be willing to kill you, but thanks be to God that the Giver of the dream is stronger than they are. Moreover, know that even while you are thinking of their well-being, they may be thinking about or plotting your destruction. Joseph and his father were thinking of giving his brothers something to eat (in other words, they were showing concern for them); yet, his brothers were rather thinking about Joseph's death.

Joseph did not understand their hate towards him. Was it because of the beautiful coat? Yes, it was one of their reasons for hating him, but that wasn't the main reason. The main reason behind their hate for him was his dream. It was simply because Joseph was able to see what God saw. Why did Potiphar's wife desire so strongly to sleep with this young man? It was because the devil saw God's greatness in Joseph so he entered into her and planned to use her to cause Joseph to go against the rules of God for his dreams to be aborted. Yes, to abort your God-given dream or vision, they will offer you things that they must not offer. Potiphar's wife offered her own body, which belonged to her husband alone, in exchange for Joseph's dream.

Anyone Who Freely Offers His or Her Body Doesn't Respect Their Body

If you're a young man or woman and you see someone whom you want to be with, beware of that person if he or she offers their body to you without thinking about the consequences that both of you will face in the presence of God. He or she might be possessed by the spirit of lust and they cannot be trusted. The truth is that, even if you want to marry each other and the other partner behaves in that manner, you must carefully consider whether you truly desire to marry the person. You must realize that they are willing to cause you to sin against God.

Today's society intensely promotes sin. There was a time when I was talking to a lady and I asked her whether she desired to keep herself pure for the Lord. She replied that, if the man wanted to sleep with her, she would do it because he might leave her if she doesn't; since everyone else is doing that. She explained that, if the man insisted, she would sleep with him. After listening to her closely, I realized just how much we have allowed the societal laws to overshadow the things and the laws of God. Yet, God will not compromise and give in to our evil ways or terms. The same lady in this situation was actually praying to God for a husband but, at the same time, she had already made up her mind about what she would do if the man were to insist that she sleep with him. She had already decided to do things her own way. It is not the will of God, and going against His will means that you are not willing to allow Him to bless you. Offering yourself to people outside the will of God does not please Him. God desires someone who will set themselves apart for Him.

Potiphar's wife gave herself freely to Joseph. Was it because she loved him? Did she care for him? Was it because she was willing to give her life for him? The answer is "NO". She was rather looking for his destruction. If you meet someone who you have even agreed to marry, what will be your reaction if that person wanted to go to bed with you before marriage? Will you take it as a sign of intense love or as a sign of destruction?

Anyone that tells you that they love you but insists on sleeping with you outside of marriage rather hates you, with a hatred from hell. Don't deceive yourself. He or she doesn't love you, because one characteristic of love is that it is patient (I Corinthians 13). You may think that this is a hard teaching but I assure you that it will help you to reach your destination. Anyone that asks you to sleep with them outside of marriage does not love you but has rather allowed themselves to be used by the enemy to rob or kill your dreams. He or she is willing to see you fall.

Sex is not a bad thing because it is ordained by God. However, it is a gift for married couples, according to the will of God. Do not allow someone to sleep with you outside of marriage because they will destroy God's plan for your life. Pre-marital sex is a covenant outside the will of God and it will have lasting effects upon you if God doesn't intervene. That is why you must practice self-control and wait to be married before having sex. Wait for the person that loves you. Anyone who loves you will wait for you. If they cannot wait for you, it means that they don't love you but rather hate you. A married person does not sleep with any other person besides their own partner. Anyone who does this is possessed by the spirit of lust and needs deliverance. But if an unmarried person truly loves you, he or she will wait for you. Everyone who truly loves you will display the love of God and have self-control towards you, not lust.

CHAPTER SIX

EVERY NEW TEST BRINGS NEW PROMOTION

Every test in your life is an opportunity for new things and new promotions. Joseph's first major test was the time he was sold. His brothers sold him, although he had not sinned against them. He was sold to the Ishmaelites who also sold him to Potiphar (Gen 39:1). He went to Egypt as a slave and served in Potiphar's house. There, the blessings of God upon his life began to affect the house. Potiphar discovered that the Lord was with him and placed many responsibilities into his hands, but soon he faced another test. Although Joseph was very comfortable in Potiphar's house, his comfort there was not the reason why God sent him to Egypt. The second test occurred to get him out of Potiphar's house, in other words, to get him out of his comfort zone. He was sent to serve in the prison.

Know that no test will come your way that will be too difficult for you to pass. The Lord knows how much you can handle, that is also why you must count it pure joy, as it is written in *James 1:2-3 NKJV, " My brethren, count it all joy when you fall into various trials, knowing that the testing of your faith produces patience."*

No Test Will Kill You If It's from God

Many times when we are tested, we often feel that the test is more than we can handle. However, God knows your strength and He will not allow you to be tested or tempted beyond your ability. It might be tough, but God knows how to deliver you. Every test that is from God has a purpose and is connected to your destiny in some way. Joseph's sentence to prison had a divine purpose. It was there in the prison that the Lord connected him to the right person. In every situation, if you allow God, He will use that situation to work for your good because He foreknew you and chose you for His divine purpose.

Roman 8:28-30 NKJV

28 And we know that all things work together for good to those who love God, to those who are the called according to His purpose.
29 For whom He foreknew, He also predestined to be conformed to the image of His Son, that He might be the firstborn among many brethren.
30 Moreover whom He predestined, these He also called; whom He called, these He also justified; and whom He justified, these He also glorified.

Regardless of how rough the test may seem, you must lift up your eyes to Calvary for your help will come from the Lord.

You Need Courage & Boldness

Joshua 1:6 NKJV" Be strong and of good courage, for to this people you shall divide as an inheritance the land which I swore to their fathers to give them."

1 Samuel 30:66 NKJV " Now David was greatly distressed, for the people spoke of stoning him, because the soul of all the people was grieved, every man for his sons and his daughters. But David strengthened himself in the Lord his God.".

Courage becomes a great factor during the tough seasons of our lives. Remember that your faith must be challenged. Joseph's faith in the Lord was challenged. Yet, because of the courage that he gathered in the Lord, he was able to stand. What you need to do is to gather courage because your courage will help you to conquer the spirit of fear in the time of trouble and it will help you to remain standing. God desires for us to be courageous. Without courage, all that is left is fear and fear only leads to failure. God instructed Joshua to be bold and courageous to stand in the test of time. From the time Joseph was sold and even when he went into prison, he kept his eyes fixed on the Lord and encouraged himself in the Lord. It is because of this courage that he was victorious. (*Genesis 39*) (*1 Samuel 30*)

If you don't encourage yourself in the Lord, many situations will kill you before your time; but, as a child of God, don't allow that to happen. Don't die before your time. King David, in 1 Samuel 30, could have died before his time because his own people wanted to kill (stone) him; but he encouraged himself and found strength in the Lord and was able to stand. Likewise, the joy of the Lord was Joseph's strength. So, even in the prison, he still made himself available for God to work through him.

Do Not Allow Circumstances to Limit the Grace of God

The grace of God was upon Joseph's life even while he was in prison. Even there, he did not cease to operate in his gifts. Many times, when we are tested and, especially, when we are in a place or situation where we don't expect to find ourselves, we allow sadness to overpower us to the point that the grace of God bestowed upon us cannot even work any longer.

Joseph, despite his situation, remained in the Lord and still operated in his grace even in the prison. In prison, he interpreted the dreams of many. You need to recognize that it is because of the grace of God upon your life that people are persecuting you. However, it is the same grace of God and the covenant that we have with Him that He will use in our deliverance. So do not stop operating in your gifts when you face many problems. Continue to work out the gift of God in your life and God will use the same grace to bring you out.

Joseph's Interpretation

Genesis 40:8-23 KJV

"8 And they said to him, "We each have had a dream, and there is no interpreter of it."

So Joseph said to them, "Do not interpretations belong to God? Tell them to me, please."

9 Then the chief butler told his dream to Joseph, and said to him, "Behold, in my dream a vine was before me, 10 and in the vine were three branches; it was as though it budded, its blossoms shot forth, and its clusters brought forth ripe grapes. 11 Then Pharaoh's cup was in my hand; and I took the grapes and pressed them into Pharaoh's cup, and placed the cup in Pharaoh's hand."

12 And Joseph said to him, "This is the interpretation of it: The three branches are three days. 13 Now within three days Pharaoh will lift up your head and restore you to your place, and you will put Pharaoh's cup in his hand according to the former manner, when you were his butler. 14 But remember me when it is well with you, and please show kindness to me; make mention of me to Pharaoh, and get me out of this house. 15 For indeed I was stolen away from the land of the Hebrews; and also I have done nothing here that they should put me into the dungeon."

16 When the chief baker saw that the interpretation was good, he said to Joseph, "I also was in my dream, and there were three white baskets on my head. 17 In the uppermost basket wereall kinds of baked goods for Pharaoh, and the birds ate them out of the basket on my head."

18 So Joseph answered and said, "This is the interpretation of it: The three baskets are three days. 19 Within three days Pharaoh will lift off your head from you and hang you on a tree; and the birds will eat your flesh from you."

20 Now it came to pass on the third day, which was Pharaoh's birthday, that he made a feast for all his servants; and he lifted up the head of the chief butler and of the chief baker among his servants. 21 Then he restored the chief butler to his butlership again, and he placed the cup in Pharaoh's hand. 22 But he hanged the chief baker, as Joseph had

*interpreted to them. 23 Yet the chief butler did not remember Joseph,
but forgot him."*

**Hardship and God's Grace: When God's Grace Is Alive and Working
in Your Life, You Possess Everything.**

2 Corinthians 6:10 NKJV
*as sorrowful, yet always rejoicing; as poor, yet making many rich; as
having nothing, and yet possessing all things.*

When God's grace is still active or alive and working, you lack
nothing. Joseph's brothers, who were the vision-killers, thought he was
finished after they sold him to Egypt. They reported that an animal had
devoured him. When God blesses you, animals may devour you yet you will
still live.

2 Corinthians 6:1-13 NKJV
*1 "We then, as workers together with Him also plead with you not to
receive the grace of God in vain.*
2 For He says: "In an acceptable time I have heard you,
And in the day of salvation I have helped you."
Behold, now is the accepted time; behold, now is the day of salvation.
3 We give no offense in anything, that our ministry may not be
blamed. 4 But in all things we commend ourselves as ministers of God: in
much patience, in tribulations, in needs, in distresses, 5 in stripes, in
imprisonments, in tumults, in labors, in sleeplessness, in fastings; 6 by
purity, by knowledge, by longsuffering, by kindness, by the Holy Spirit,
by sincere love, 7 by the word of truth, by the power of God, by the armor
of righteousness on the right hand and on the left, 8 by honor and
dishonor, by evil report and good report; as deceivers, and yettrue; 9 as
unknown, and yet well known; as dying, and behold we live; as chastened,

and yet *not killed; 10 as sorrowful, yet always rejoicing; as poor, yet making many rich; as having nothing, and* yet *possessing all things.*

His brothers thought that selling him would be the end of his story. They did not realize that selling Joseph did not mean they could sell his gift or destiny. Know that the gift to fulfill your prophetic destiny is eternal and the greatest gift we have been given is the gift of Christ, the Holy Spirit, through whom the other gifts operate. If you have the Holy Spirit, who is the greatest gift, you lack nothing. If you have the grace of God (who is Jesus Christ), then you truly have everything.

Romans 6:22-23 NKJV "But now having been set free from sin, and having become slaves of God, you have your fruit to holiness, and the end, everlasting life. For the wages of sin is death, but the gift of God is eternal life in Christ Jesus our Lord."

Romans 8:32 NKJV "He who did not spare His own Son, but delivered Him up for us all, how shall He not with Him also freely give us all things?"

In all, Joseph didn't lose the presence of God, because it is written that God was with him. He still had the presence, which is the Holy Spirit. Regardless of what you have lost physically, if you have Jesus, then you don't lack anything. Joseph hadn't lost anything at all. He still had what would lead to the manifestation of his dream. Potiphar's wife thought she could end his life in prison because he refused to sleep with her, but his life could not end there because he still had the gift of God. God prepared a table before him in the presence of his accuser. What matters is that the gift of God (the Holy Spirit) is the link to your destiny and He will deliver you from all troubles.

Genesis 40:14 NKJV " But remember me when it is well with you, and please show kindness to me; make mention of me to Pharaoh, and get me out of this house.".

Joseph knew that he was a Hebrew who was forcibly sold to a foreign land. He knew that he did not deserve to be in prison and, so, certainly God would deliver him. I believe that the cupbearer went to prison because of Joseph. Sometimes, because of us and our dreams, God will cause certain events to happen in the lives of others so that we would be linked with our vision helpers.

The Grace of God Cannot Be Imprisoned

No one can subdue the gift of God upon your life. They can place you in an uncomfortable place like prison, but the gift of God cannot be chained. Joseph was in prison but the Lord was with him every day. It was the grace of God that delivered him out of the prison. Yes, grace is able to deliver you. The gift of God upon your life is able to deliver. The gift of God upon your life can set you free. No one can chain your prayer life. They may be able to prevent you from reading the Bible, but they cannot stop you from meditating on the Word of God every day and night. They can arise against you and the grace of God upon your life, but they cannot prevail against the Word of God, because the Word is greater than destruction and hindrances. The Word of God cannot be chained. Paul and Silas were in prison chains, yet the Word could not be chained. They even sang praises that night and there was an earthquake. The chains were broken and the shackles were taken away. The foundation of the prison shook because the power within the Word was not restrained. They exercised the power of the Word by singing songs of praise and hymns and God brought deliverance (Acts 16:16-40).

Every Dream Is Under Attack

If you are a dreamer, then expect attacks because every gift of God is under attack. The attacks come from Satan, but he recruits people as his agents to execute it. The evil spirits do not want you to see God's dream manifest in your life. Remember that Joseph was a threat to the kingdom of hell. Joseph was under attack before he was even born. Jesus went through the same process and situation and so was Moses. When God has given you a gift, you must know that you are under attack. They will attack but they will not be able to prevail against you.

You Are Your Dream

No one is greater than their dream because, as a man thinks in his heart, so he is. The devil is against anyone who has a dream because when there's revelation, there's redemption; but when revelation is lost, everything becomes chaotic. That is why the devil hates dreamers because he knows that, if he allows you to confirm what the Lord has said about you, you will do exploit. Thus, he will attack you and the dream. Again, you must recognize that every Godly dream is under attack. The devil and his followers are aware that what you can see and confirm with God is what you will receive. Whatever you dream is what you will become. They hated Joseph, sold him, lied against him, and cast him into prison. All of this was done to fight against his dream. However, with the Lord's help, he was able to see his dream come to pass and he became what he envisioned. The question is, do you have a dream? If so, what is your dream and is it a positive dream? Is that dream from God or is it a product of your own imagination? Is it a dream you envisioned on your own or did you seek the face of God about it? Let your dream fit into God's perfect will for your life and God will cause you to fulfill your dream.

Genesis 41:38-45 NKJV

"38 And Pharaoh said to his servants, "Can we find such a one as this, a man in whom is the Spirit of God?"

39 Then Pharaoh said to Joseph, "Inasmuch as God has shown you all this, there is no one as discerning and wise as you. 40 You shall be over my house, and all my people shall be ruled according to your word; only in regard to the throne will I be greater than you." 41 And Pharaoh said to Joseph, "See, I have set you over all the land of Egypt."

42 Then Pharaoh took his signet ring off his hand and put it on Joseph's hand; and he clothed him in garments of fine linen and put a gold chain around his neck. 43 And he had him ride in the second chariot which he had; and they cried out before him, "Bow the knee!" So he set him over all the land of Egypt. 44 Pharaoh also said to Joseph, "I am Pharaoh, and without your consent no man may lift his hand or foot in all the land of Egypt." 45 And Pharaoh called Joseph's name Zaphnath-Paaneah. And he gave him as a wife Asenath, the daughter of Poti-Pherah priest of On. So Joseph went out over all the land of Egypt."

Pharaoh said to Joseph, "I hereby put you in charge of the whole land of Egypt". He put his own signet ring on Joseph's finger, dressed him in robes of fine linen, and put a gold chain around his neck. He even made him ride on a chariot as his second-in-command and men shouted before him, "Make Way!". Moreover, he put him in charge of the whole land of Egypt. At long last, Joseph realized his dream. Everything he dreamt about came to pass. Praise God! Your dream is about to come to pass in the name of Jesus!

Prayer

May you be the next person to be clothed, to be promoted, and to have the King's ring. May the glory of Jehovah God take you from where you are to a higher level and may God surely raise you up to actualize your dreams and to become who He created you to become, in Jesus' name.

Don't give up on your dreams, for your destiny is becoming a reality and you will live to fulfill your life's purpose.

CHAPTER SEVEN

GOD HAS THE FINAL SAY IN YOUR SCHOOL OF JOSEPH

God has the final say in your life. It doesn't matter how rough and tough it may seem, what God has purposed is what will stand. God kept quiet for Joseph to go through all these trials, yet none of them was able to change the purpose of God. I believe that it was because of Joseph that the king cupbearer also went to prison. The cupbearer had a dream because of Joseph and, because of Joseph, Pharaoh had a dream that no one could interpret. The dream was meant for Joseph alone to interpret. Just think of it. How could a king seek after a slave in prison, attend to him, put a ring on his finger, place him on a chariot and cause him to be recognized as the second in command in a foreign land? This was the doing of the Lord. Praise God! What God said to Joseph finally came to pass because He, God, has the final say.

Psalm 105:17-22 KJV

"17 He sent a man before them, even Joseph, who was sold for a servant:

18 Whose feet they hurt with fetters: he was laid in iron:

19 Until the time that his word came: the word of the Lord tried him.

20 The king sent and loosed him; even the ruler of the people, and let him go free.

21 He made him lord of his house, and ruler of all his substance:

22 To bind his princes at his pleasure; and teach his senators wisdom."

School of Joseph

Everybody will have to go through "The School of Joseph" in one way or another. Now, I want to tell you a true story about the school of Joseph that a certain young man endured. For privacy reasons, we will call him, Luke. According to his mother's testimony, on the very day of his birth, she had a dream that some people were seeking to cut her tongue with a saw. When Luke was between the age of 5 to 7 years old, she dreamt again and she saw three women with their faces covered putting him on fire to burn him alive. In that dream, she fought them and asked them why they wanted to put a living human being on a fire to burn him alive. Their reply to her was, "His father said he is cold." So, she took him from their hands through a struggle and a fight.

Exactly 2 weeks after that dream, Luke began to suffer from an inexplicable illness that occurred periodically. Whenever the illness would occur, he experienced painful sensations as if someone was pulling his veins and breaking his bones. Despite its severity, no doctor was able to diagnose the illness. Almost every 2 weeks, he had to be admitted to the hospital and was subsequently scheduled for follow-ups every two weeks.

Predictably, the continual illnesses disrupted his education. It became serious to the point that he could not attend his classes regularly from elementary school to high school. He attended school as his strength permitted him. Because of the report from his doctors, the school authorities just abided by the conditions set for him by his doctors. Despite the challenges, Luke was a bright student. However, his situation worsened, and his condition took a turn for the worst. Three separate times, he became unconscious and, in one of those events, he even fell into a coma. At a certain point in time when the doctors were giving him blood, it began to come from his nose and mouth at the same time while he was still unconscious.

It came to a point that the doctors were not sure whether or not he would wake up, but the power of God revived him again. Because of his condition, the doctors thought it possible that he might die before the age of 18. However, it is the Lord who controls the power of death and he was able to live and is still alive today. These spiritual attacks were so great upon his life but he was able to win the battle because the Lord was with him.

The attacks, however, continued. He was taken to different places and churches to see if he could be healed. Yet, he did not receive healing and because of the constant and unbearable pain that he was suffering, he attempted to take his life many times. He even prayed to God to take his life, yet, the Lord spared him. It was the Word of God alone that prevented him from taking his life.

As time went along, he joined a group prayer meeting. There, however, he saw his illnesses worsen as the group increased their prayers. His sicknesses intensified to the extent that he had to be admitted to the hospital while his peers were writing their Junior High School exams. Yet he remained hopeful in the Lord and asked his doctors for permission to go and write his exams. Eventually, as the prayers continued to intensify, his sicknesses begun to subside and he was healed by the power of God. Unfortunately, after he got well from the chronic illnesses, he also suffered a serious injury to his right leg which caused him continuous pain for many years. Doctors could not discover what the problem was. All they could say about his leg was that there was a hole in his right hip.

After High School, Luke decided to follow the call of God upon his life to work for God and preach the gospel despite all the challenges. By then, he had received many prophetic utterances from multiple men of God who confirmed the call of ministry upon his life. Since he was 12 years old, he had been preaching in the marketplaces, bus stations, churches, and radio stations, as he got the opportunity and as he was directed by the Lord.

At that time, he also began to face trials from family members to a point that he realized that continuing the work of God would mean that he would no longer receive any support from his family. Yet, Luke did not give up on his God. He trusted that God would meet his every need. He continued to preach through the pains of his affected leg. Eventually, God miraculously opened a door for him to travel twice. However, not having the funds to complete the necessary documents, he was unable to do so.

Several years later, God opened yet another door for him. Miraculously, someone he had not previously known decided to sponsor him to travel to the United States of America. In the U.S., he faced some of the toughest trials he had ever experienced in his life. God revealed to Luke three times through visions and dreams that there will be attacks upon his life because some individuals back in his home country had risen up against him. They had recited incantations and planned to either kill him or destroy his life through spiritual attacks. Furthermore, he received several phone calls confirming that some threats had been made against his life. A few days after these things were revealed to him, he began to face difficulties with his health again. However, as he had done in times past, Luke turned his eyes towards the Lord. Through his continual prayers and several hospital visitations, he regained his strength.

Again, Luke experienced another trial in his School of Joseph. A woman in the church began to claim that God told her that Luke will marry her and become her husband. Since he didn't respond favorably to her, she took it to another level. Because of his refusal to accept her proposal and that her claim was from God, she began to speak badly about him in public. She even reported him to the Senior Pastor, claiming that God had spoken to her and that Luke had also given her hope that they would marry one day.

As a result, he was disciplined by the church without any proper investigation by the leaders of the church, although he had done nothing wrong. The pastors never sought the face of the Lord to confirm the allegations. His punishment was that, for six months, he could no longer preach nor participate in any church activities. He wasn't allowed to lead anything in the church. Although exclusion from participating in the communion was normally a part of the punishments of that church, he refused to exclude himself and continued to participate in the regular communion service. All these trials came purposely to extinguish the call of God upon his life just as the attacks on Joseph's life came purposely to destroy his dream.

What I am trying to say is that even when you set your heart on the things of God you will face terrible attacks. Know that the people, being used by the devil, may even claim that God had spoken to them. Be prepared that there will be people who will insist that you fulfill their will instead of the Lord's. To persuade you to do their will, they may even claim that the Lord has spoken to them. If you refuse, they may even go as far as attempting to tarnish or destroy your reputation and your ministry.

Why should the lovers of God have to go through such terrible times in their lives? Does God not appreciate their work? Hasn't God seen all the work that they have done for Him? God sees all your works but knows that He will use the school of Joseph to promote you to another level if you pass your test. That is why God permits them.

Joseph Experience

All the above are some examples of the difficulties you could face as a man or woman of God. Remember that your trial will most definitely come in a different form. Joseph endured all these difficulties but, at the end of it all, God glorified him and his name. What is your School of Joseph? Which things are you facing that are too difficult for you? Do not depend on your own strength, but the Lord's.

Like Joseph went to prison after being wrongfully accused, Jesus was crucified without cause. In every trial you face where you have been wrongfully accused, remember that the truth cannot be hidden or covered forever. Truth is a Spirit. Truth is a personality. The Truth is the person of Christ. You cannot hide the Truth, you cannot hide Jesus Christ. Even if you burry Him, He will spring forth again eventually. The Truth will set you free.

John 8:32 NKJV "And you shall know the truth, and the truth shall make you free."

Luke 8:17 NKJV "For nothing is secret that will not be revealed, nor anything hidden that will not be known and come to light."

Ecclesiastes 12:4 NKJV "For God shall bring every work into judgment, with every secret thing, whether it be good, or whether it be evil."

Remember that God is your helper. Look to Him and He will see you through, even in the difficult times. It is my prayer that you will be like Joseph and that you may come out of prison. I pray that God will lift up your heads. May your enemies not be able to look at your face on the day that you come out!

There is a need for young pastors who are unmarried, both men and women, to be careful because many people will come pretending as if they need your help; but, sometimes, it is only a plan from the enemy to use them to cause your downfall and to bring down your ministry.

Prayer

If, by any means, the enemy has lied against you and it has cost you something, even prison, may God surely visit you and deliver you, because the Truth cannot be bound. May you be set free, in Jesus' name! May God bless you because of what you have endured in your School of Joseph. May all your dreams come true. May God promote you. May you be placed in a position of command like Joseph. May God prepare a table before you in the presence of your accusers. May He declare His faithfulness upon your life because of your dreams, in Jesus' name. Amen and amen.

CHAPTER EIGHT

PRAYER

If you have not confessed Christ, you can do it now because today is your day.

I
Prayer of Confession

Say: Lord Jesus, this hour, I *(mention your name)* confess you as my personal Savior and Lord. I now invite you to come into my life (my heart), take control over my life, and give me eternal life. Write my name in the Lamb book of life and help me to walk in your perfect will all the days of my life. In Jesus' name, I pray (Romans 3:23, Romans 6:26, Romans 10:9-11), amen.

II
Prayer of Repentance

If you have allowed yourself to be used against any man or woman of God, like Potiphar's wife did, pray this prayer.

Say: Lord Jesus, I am sorry for allowing myself to be used by the devil against your servant. Now, I forsake my evil ways and I repent of my sins. Please forgive me and take your place in my heart. Devil, I lose myself from every covenant I had with you; every spirit-, soul-, and body-tie. You have no part in me because I have repented of my sins and my evil ways. I have given my life to Jesus Christ and He is my Lord. Christ is my Savior and my redeemer, and I will forever be His. In Jesus' name, I pray, Amen and amen. (1 John 1:5-9. 1 John 2:9-12).

III
Prayer of Strength, Empowerment, and Breakthrough

If you are a man or woman of God who has experienced the school of Joseph in your life and you are disturbed or distressed as a result of what you have faced, pray this prayer.

Say: Lord Jesus, through your strength, I am more, than a conqueror.

I thank you for giving me the strength to stand and I declare that I have become victorious over the schemes of Satan. Continue to empower me, anoint my head with fresh oil and shame my enemies. Exalt me like you exalted Joseph in the land of Egypt and bless all that I do. May my dreams come true. In Jesus' name, amen and amen (1 John 2:13-14. Psalm 105:17-22).

IV

Prayer of Deliverance and Restoration

This prayer is for those who were not able to stand when they faced trials and tests. It is for those who fell into the trap of the wicked one. Pray this prayer for God's deliverance.

Say: Lord Jesus, I pray now in the name of Jesus. I ask for forgiveness. Cleanse me, restore my life, and redeem me completely from the hands of the wicked messenger and his agents. Save my spirit, save my soul and save my body. Cause me to become the person you made me to be, in Jesus' name. Lord, do not take your Spirit from me and do not cast me away from your presence. Restore the joy of your salvation to me. For the rest of my life, give me the strength to stand against such attacks that come my way and deliver me from temptation. In Jesus' name I pray, Amen and Amen (Psalm 51; 1 John 1:5-12).

1 John 3:4-24 NKJV

⁴ Whoever commits sin also commits lawlessness, and sin is lawlessness. ⁵ And you know that He was manifested to take away our sins, and in Him there is no sin. ⁶ Whoever abides in Him does not sin. Whoever sins has neither seen Him nor known Him.

⁷ Little children, let no one deceive you. He who practices righteousness is righteous, just as He is righteous. ⁸ He who sins is of the devil, for the devil has sinned from the beginning. For this purpose the Son of God was manifested, that He might destroy the works of the devil. ⁹ Whoever has been born of God does not sin, for His seed remains in him; and he cannot sin, because he has been born of God.

¹⁰ In this the children of God and the children of the devil are manifest: Whoever does not practice righteousness is not of God, nor is he who does not love his brother. ¹¹ For this is the message that you heard from the beginning, that we should love one another, ¹² not as Cain who was of the wicked one and murdered his brother. And why did he murder him? Because his works were evil and his brother's righteous.

¹³ Do not marvel, my brethren, if the world hates you. ¹⁴ We know that we have passed from death to life, because we love the brethren. He who does not love his brother abides in death. ¹⁵ Whoever hates his brother is a murderer, and you know that no murderer has eternal life abiding in him.

¹⁶ By this we know love, because He laid down His life for us. And we also ought to lay down our lives for the brethren. ¹⁷ But whoever has this world's goods, and sees his brother in need, and shuts up his heart from him, how does the love of God abide in him?

¹⁸ My little children, let us not love in word or in tongue, but in deed and in truth. ¹⁹ And by this we know that we are of the truth, and shall assure our hearts before Him. ²⁰ For if our heart condemns us, God is greater than our heart, and knows all things. ²¹ Beloved, if our heart does not condemn us, we have confidence toward God. ²² And whatever we ask we receive from Him, because we keep His commandments and do those things that are pleasing in His sight. ²³ And this is His commandment: that we should believe on the name of His Son Jesus Christ and love one another, as He gave us commandment.

²⁴ Now he who keeps His commandments abides in Him, and He in him. And by this we know that He abides in us, by the Spirit whom He has given us.

1 John 3:8b, says that Christ came to destroy the works of the devil. So, if you want to remain in fellowship with Him, lift up your eyes to Christ

and God will turn your shame into glory. May this book minister to your heart as we study it together. The Christian life is a tough and rough one. Yet, Christ is able to take us to our destination. Be sensitive and prayerful, don't worry yourself about the sins you have not committed nor whether you have been lied against. Just fix your eyes on Christ who is the author of our faith, and He will see you through as he did for Joseph. Know that, before the glory and before the promotion, there is a test. God is about to lift you up so count it pure joy when you face difficulties, troubles, tribulation, and problems that will come your way (The Joseph School of Ministry). Even when you experience your time or form of imprisonment, God sees you. May He help you to keep the faith until Jesus returns. Amen and amen.

CHAPTER NINE

CONCLUSION

In conclusion, you must understand that, until the time that your word of fulfillment comes, the word of the LORD will try you. But, like Joseph, you must remain loyal to God and faithful to yourself. Protect the dream by staying away from evil. Make sure to do your best to pass every test and God will lift you up.

Psalm 105:16-24 NKJV

16 Moreover He called for a famine in the land;

He destroyed all the provision of bread.

17 He sent a man before them—

Joseph—who was sold as a slave.

18 They hurt his feet with fetters,

He was laid in irons.

19 Until the time that his word came to pass,

The word of the Lord tested him.

20 The king sent and released him,

The ruler of the people let him go free.

21 He made him lord of his house,

And ruler of all his possessions,

22 To bind his princes at his pleasure,

And teach his elders wisdom.

23 Israel also came into Egypt,

And Jacob dwelt in the land of Ham.

24 He increased His people greatly,

And made them stronger than their enemies.

Like Joseph, may the hand of Yahweh (the Lord) rearrange your life, change your condition for good, lift up your head, and place you in the corridor of powers. Amen and amen. May God richly bless you. Shalom.

www.ingramcontent.com/pod-product-compliance
Lightning Source LLC
Chambersburg PA
CBHW060505160726
47992CB00003B/1334